Animal Differences

Author:
Gomathy Shankaran

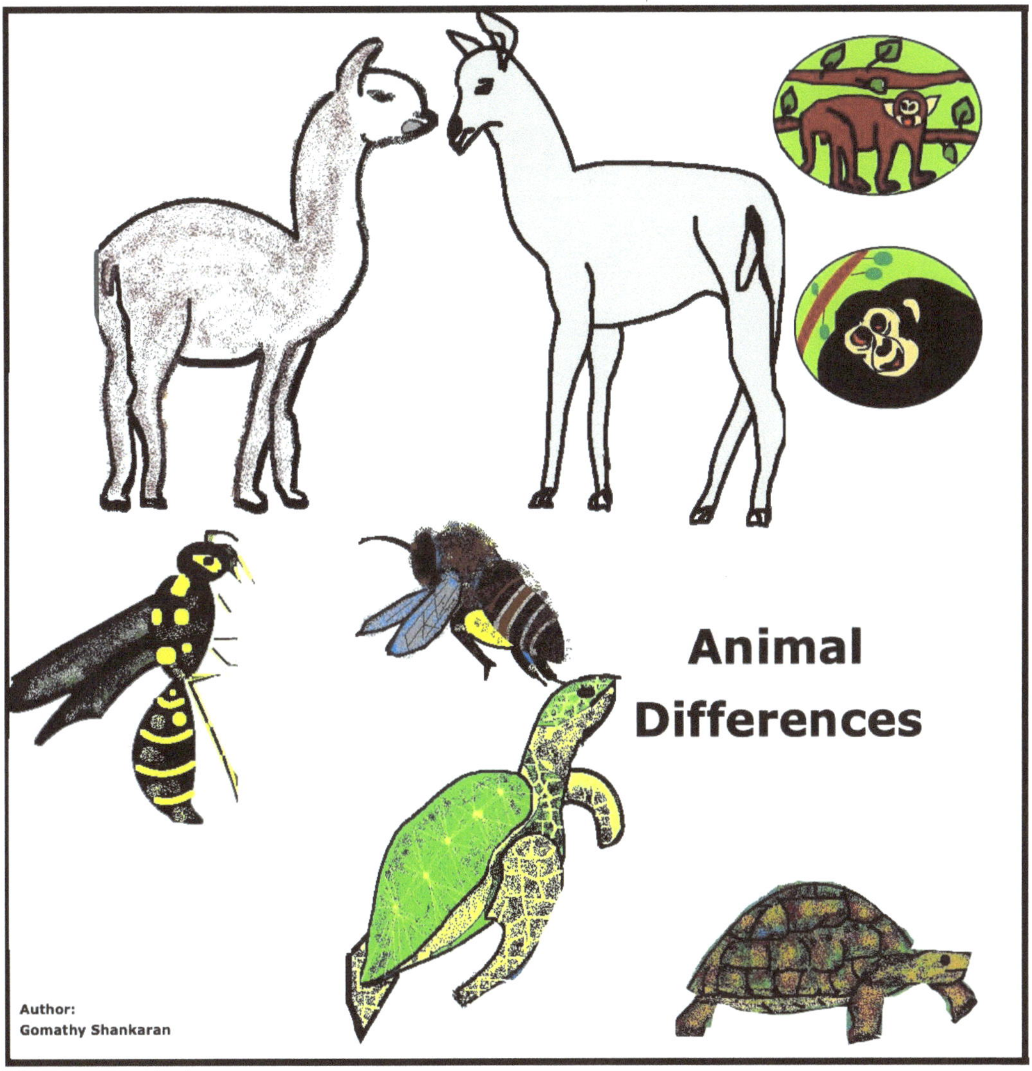

Table Of Contents

Title   Page

1: Turtle Vs Tortoise   3

2: Wasp Vs Bee   8

3: Alpaca Vs Llama   15

4: Monkey Vs Ape   23

Turtle vs Tortoise

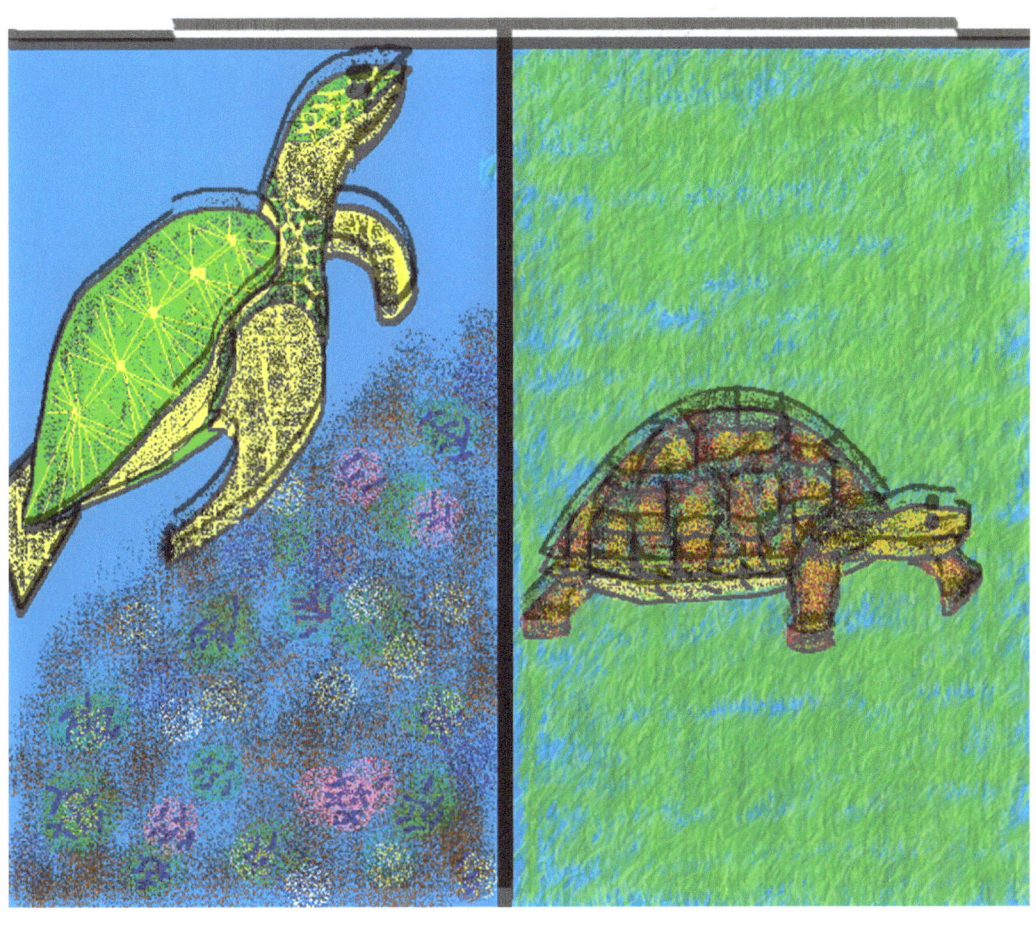

Turtles spend most of their time in water.
Tortoises live mostly on land.

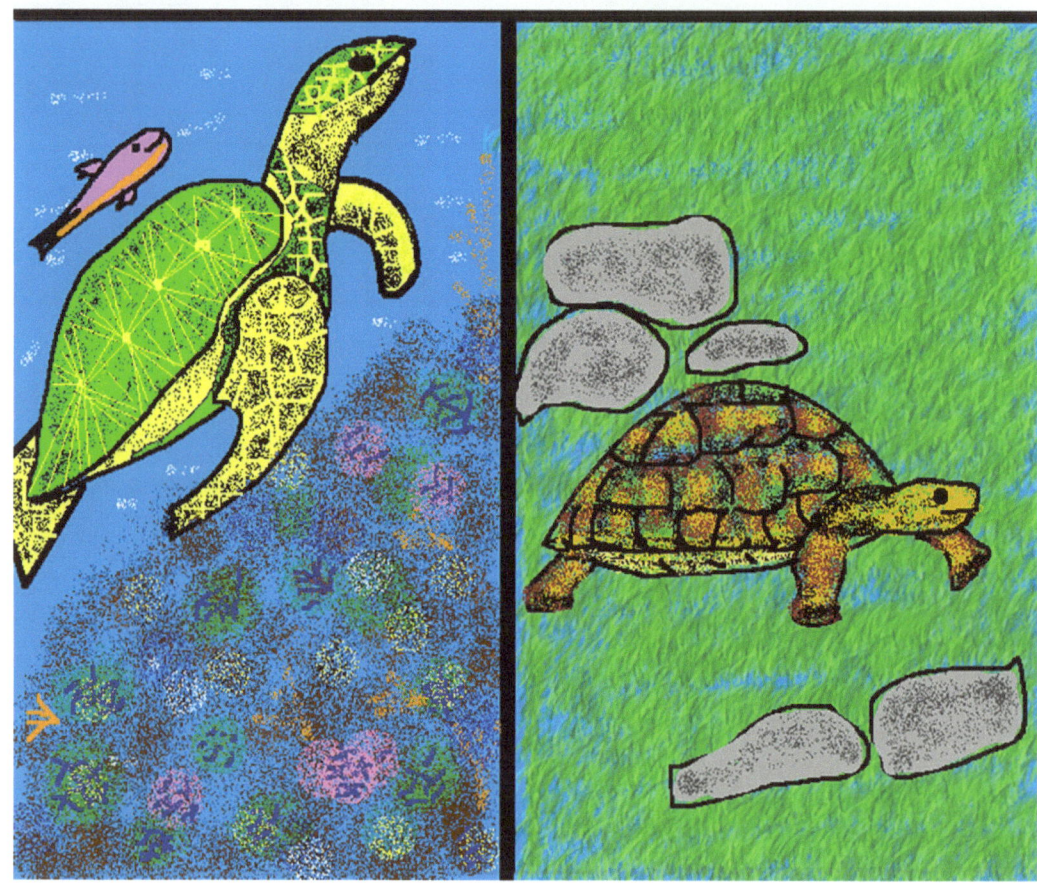

Turtles are omnivorous. They eat small worms and some plant matter. Tortoises are vegetarian.

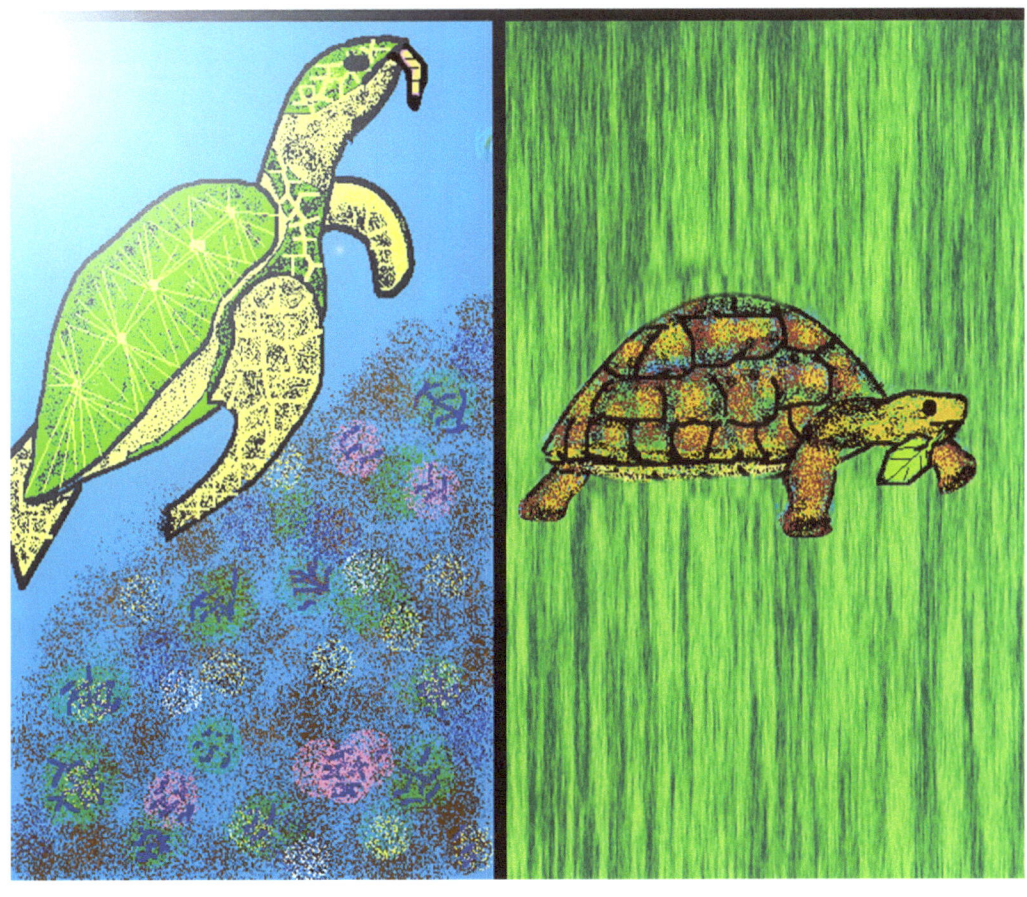

Turtles have a webbed feet to swim efficiently in water. Tortoises have pillar like hind feet.

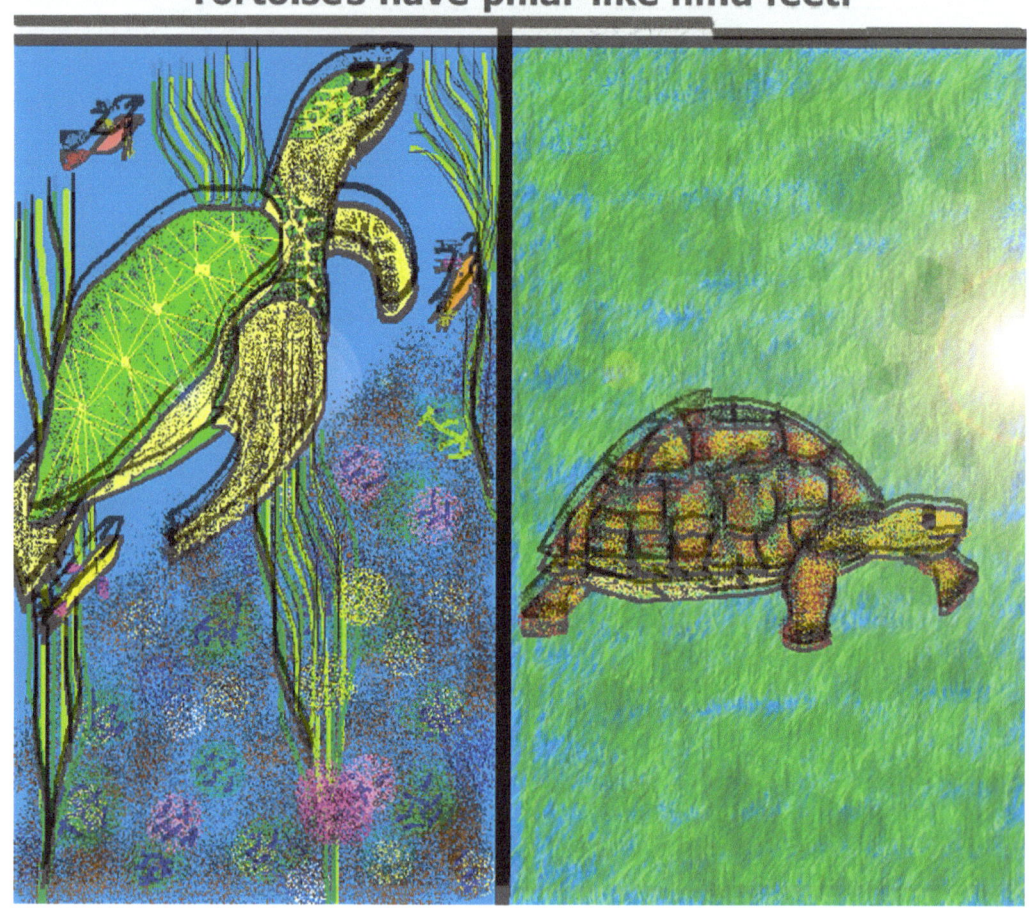

All tortoises are turtles, but not all turtles are tortoises:

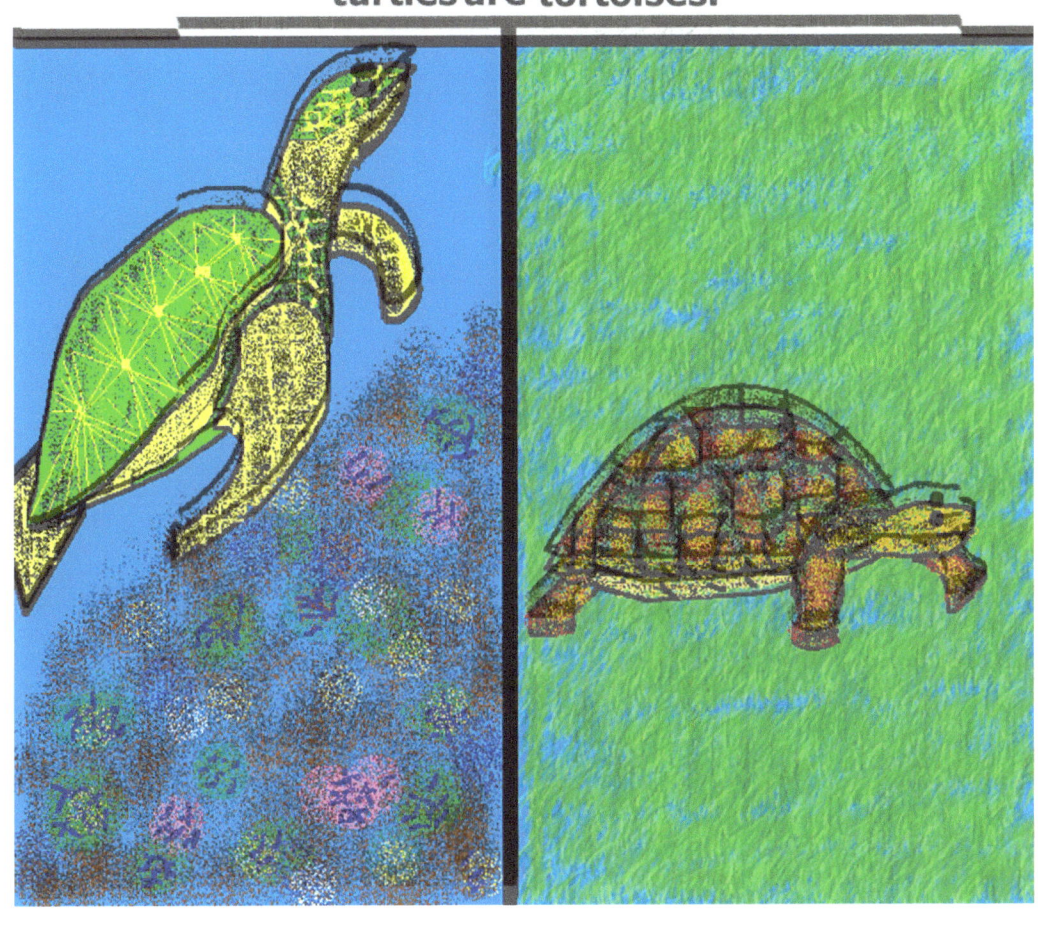

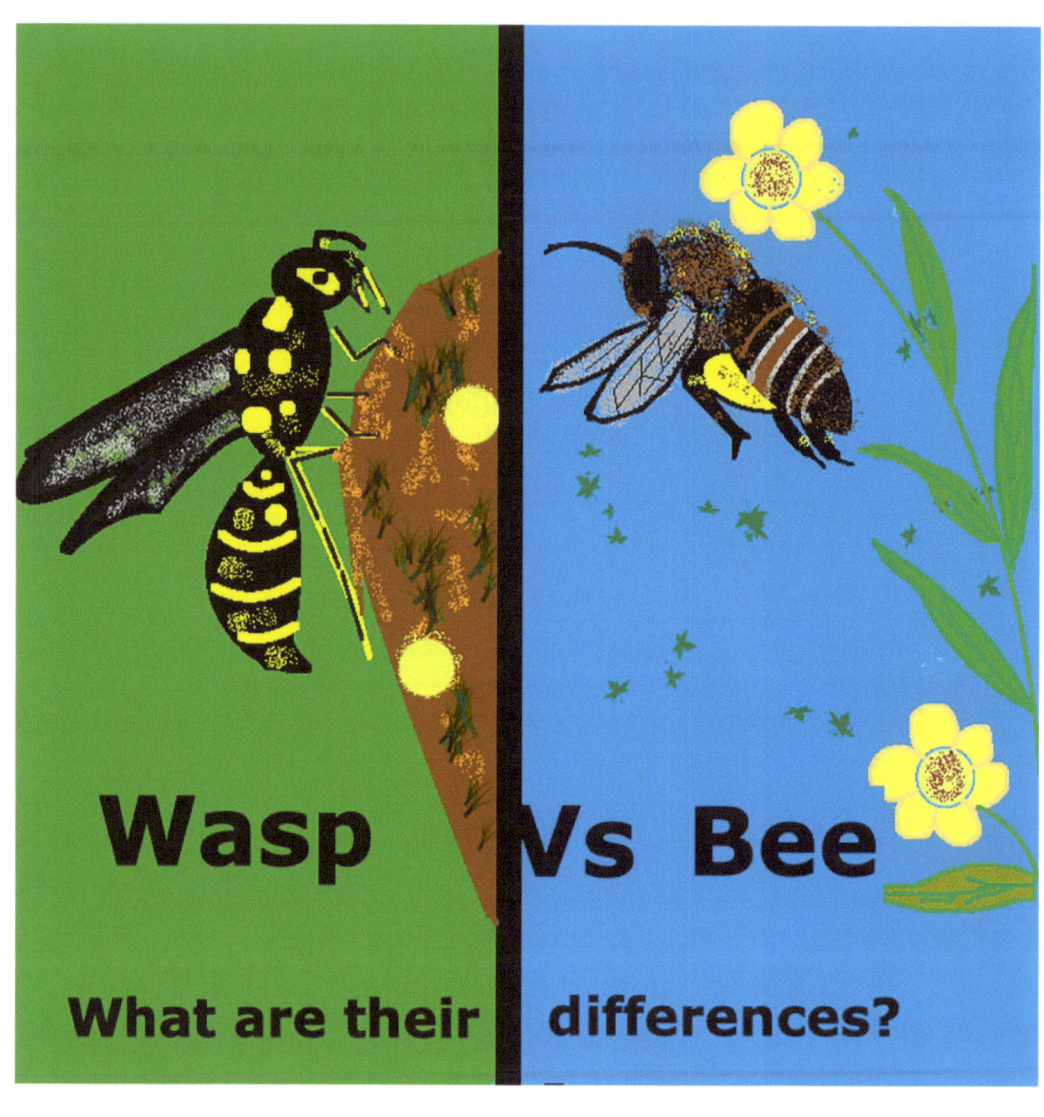

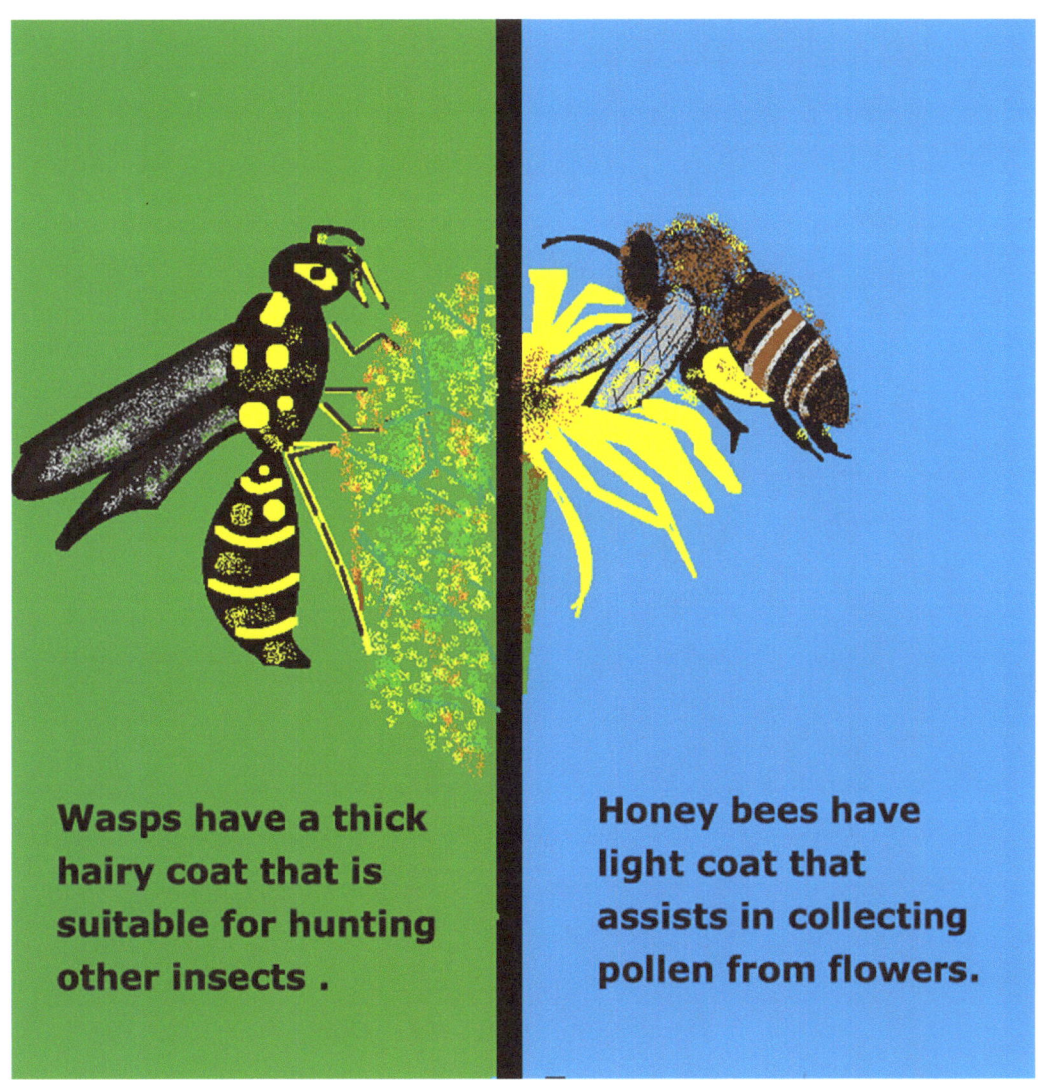

Wasps have a thick hairy coat that is suitable for hunting other insects .

Honey bees have light coat that assists in collecting pollen from flowers.

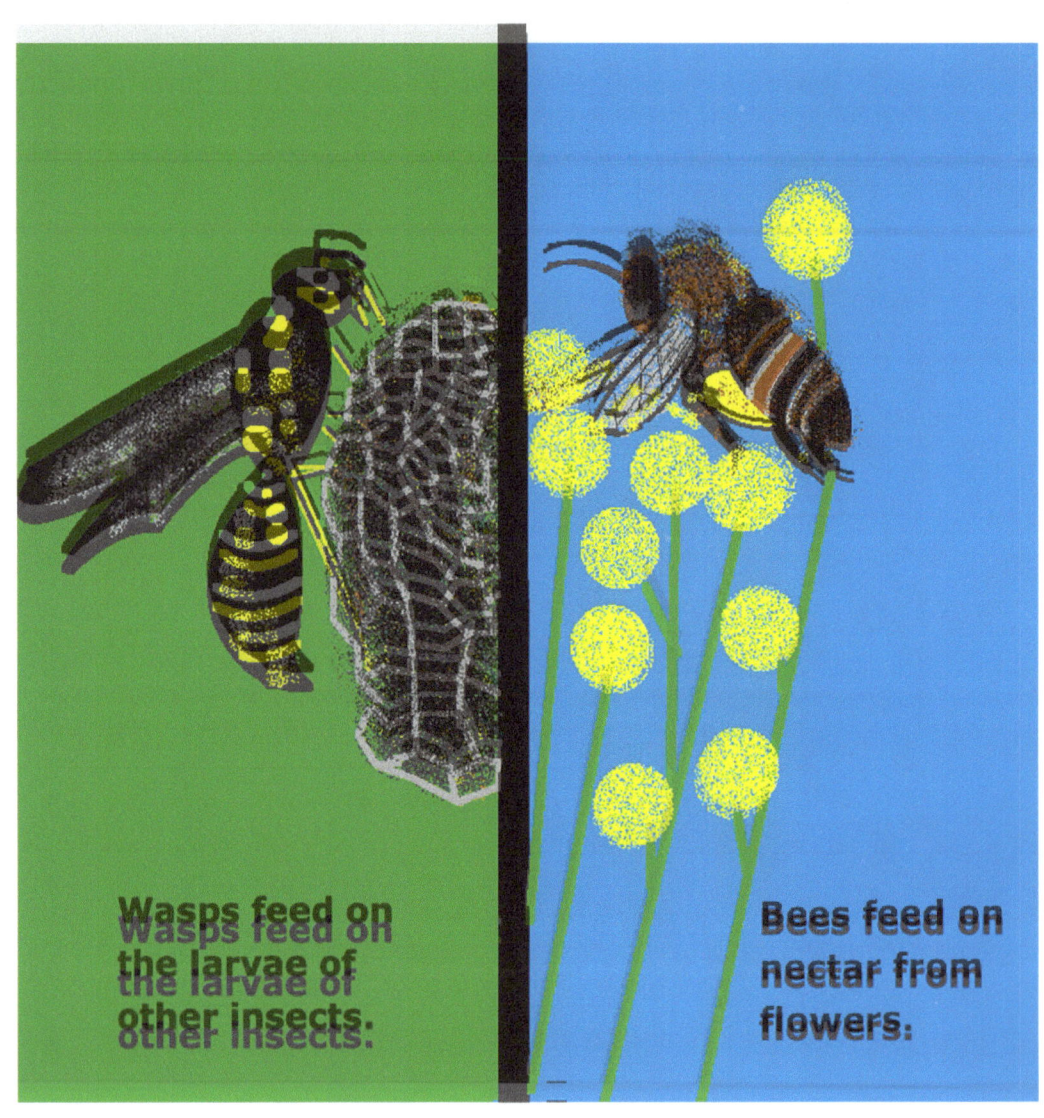

Wasps feed on the larvae of other insects.

Bees feed on nectar from flowers.

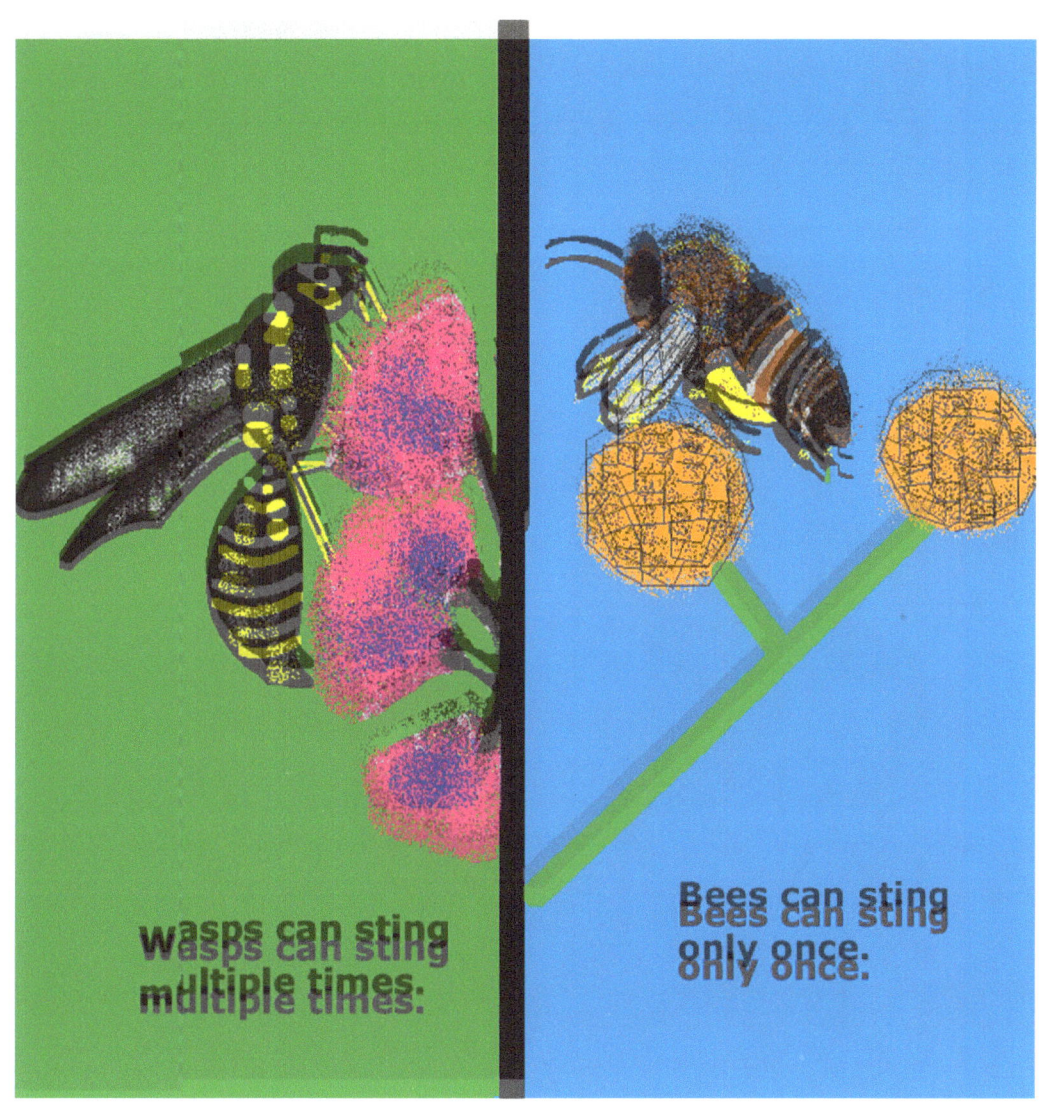

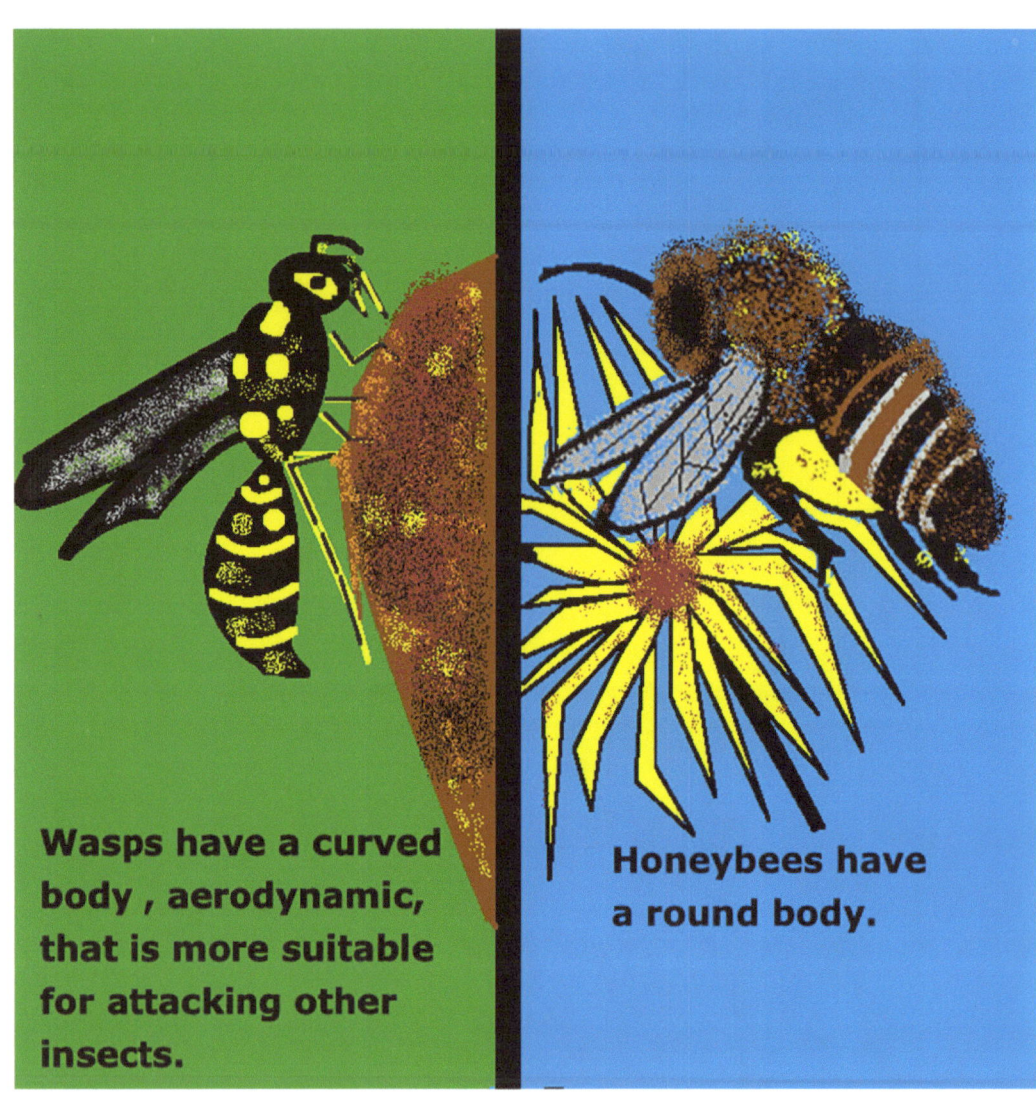

Wasps have a curved body, aerodynamic, that is more suitable for attacking other insects.

Honeybees have a round body.

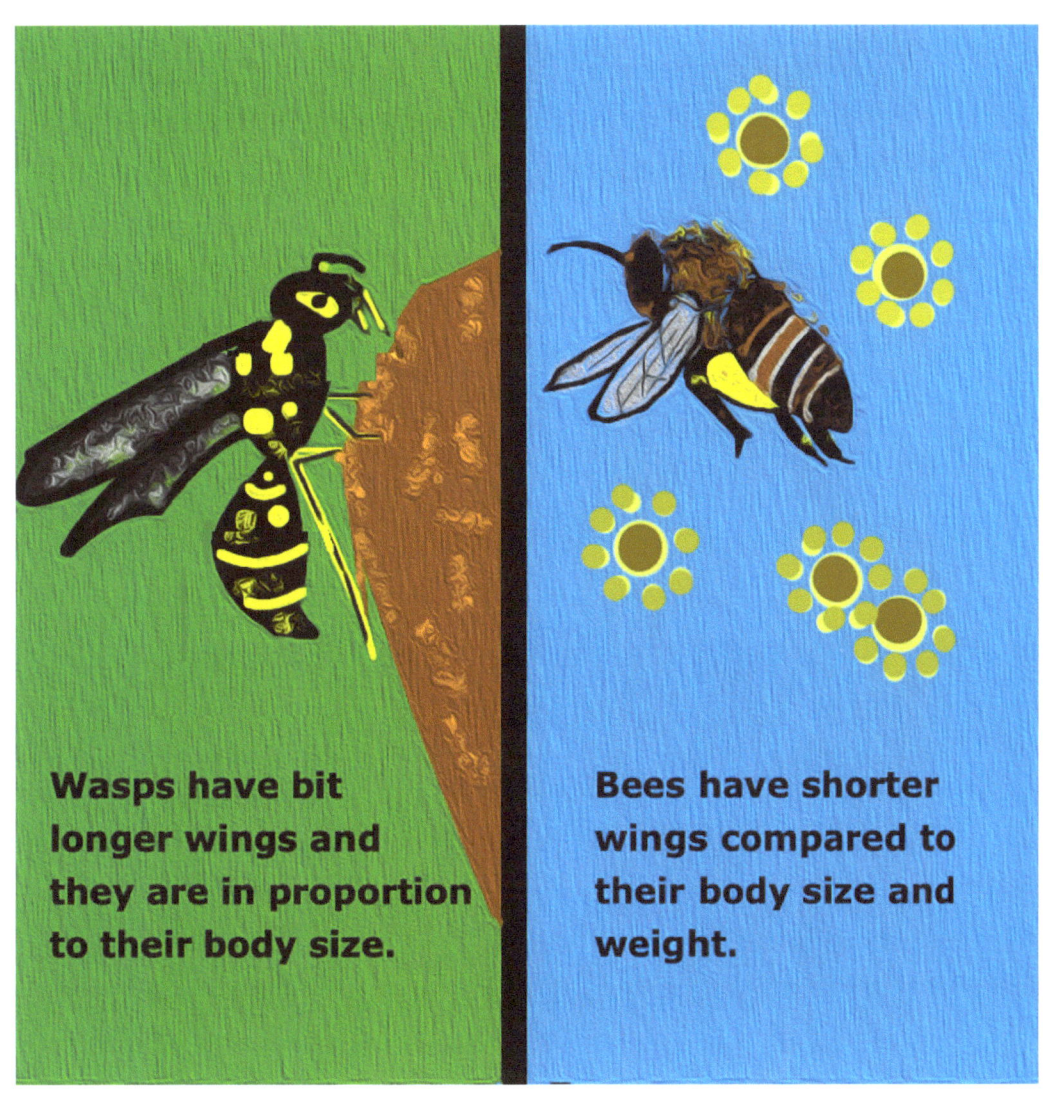

Wasps have bit longer wings and they are in proportion to their body size.

Bees have shorter wings compared to their body size and weight.

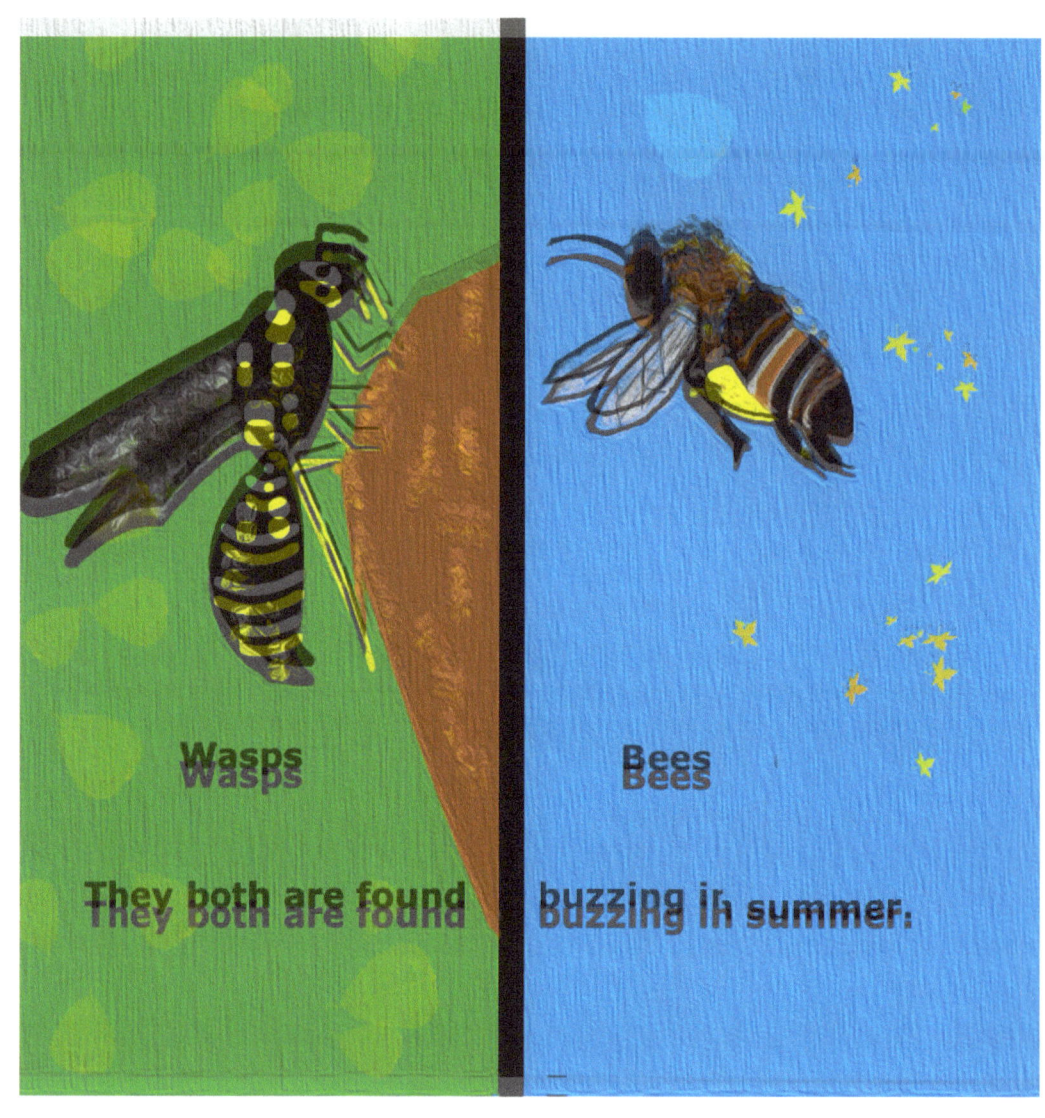

Wasps

Bees

They both are found buzzing in summer.

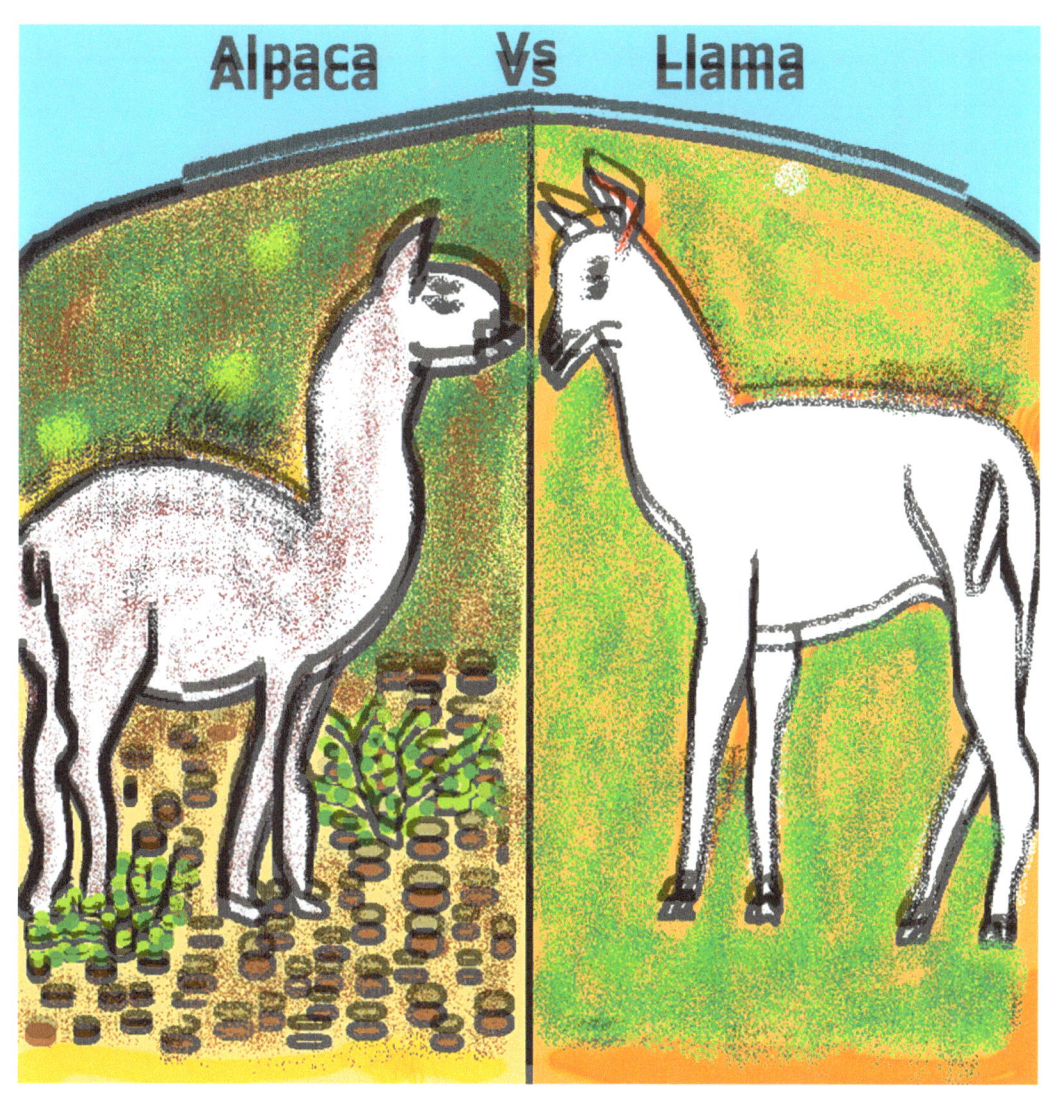

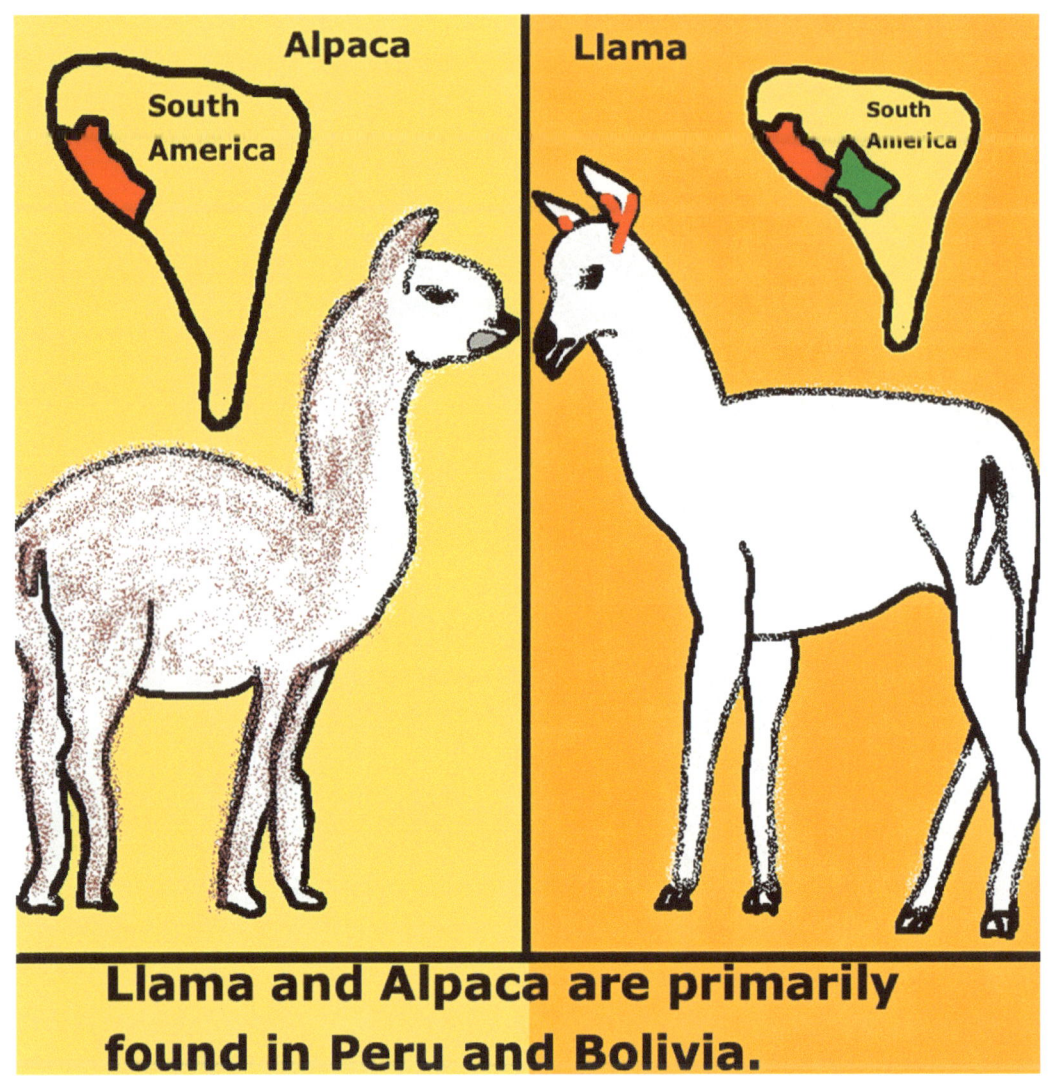

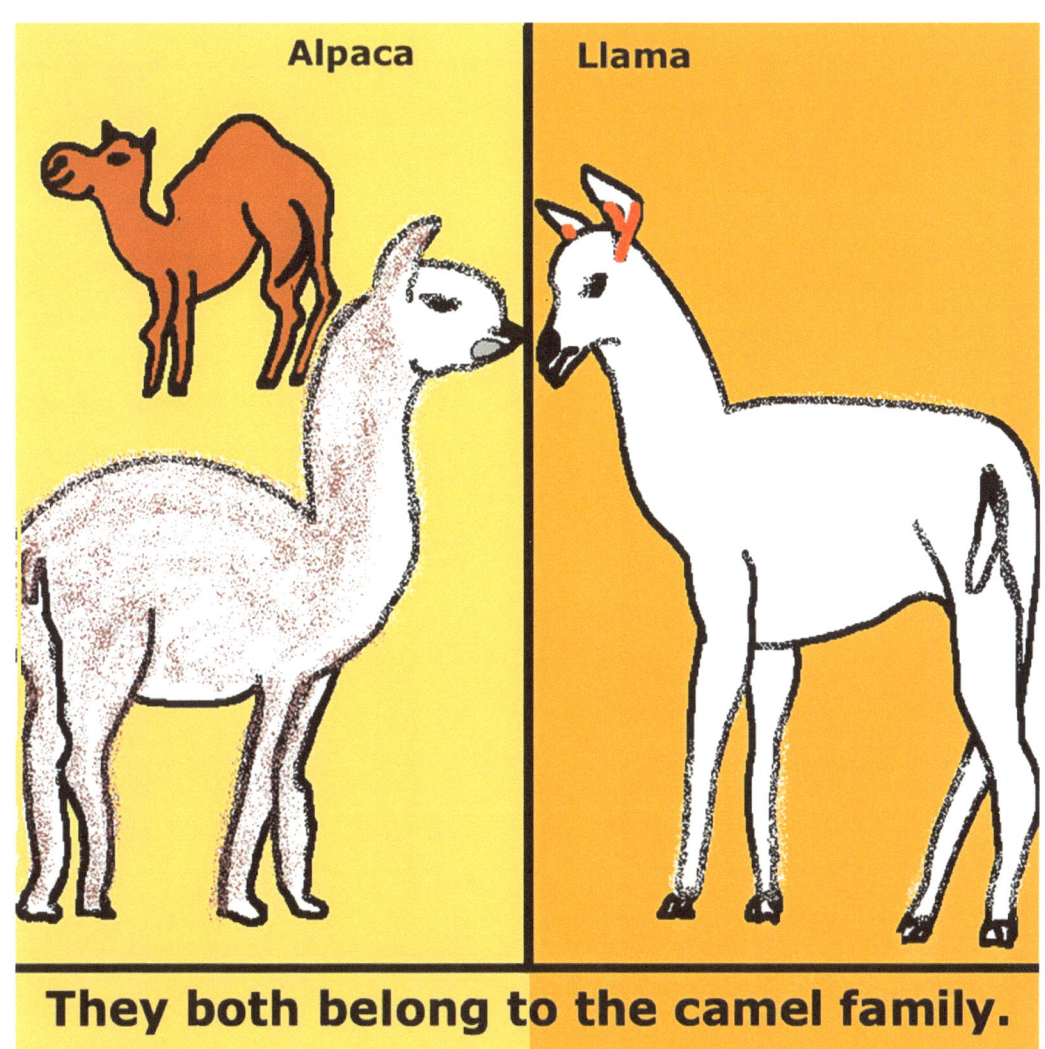

They both belong to the camel family.

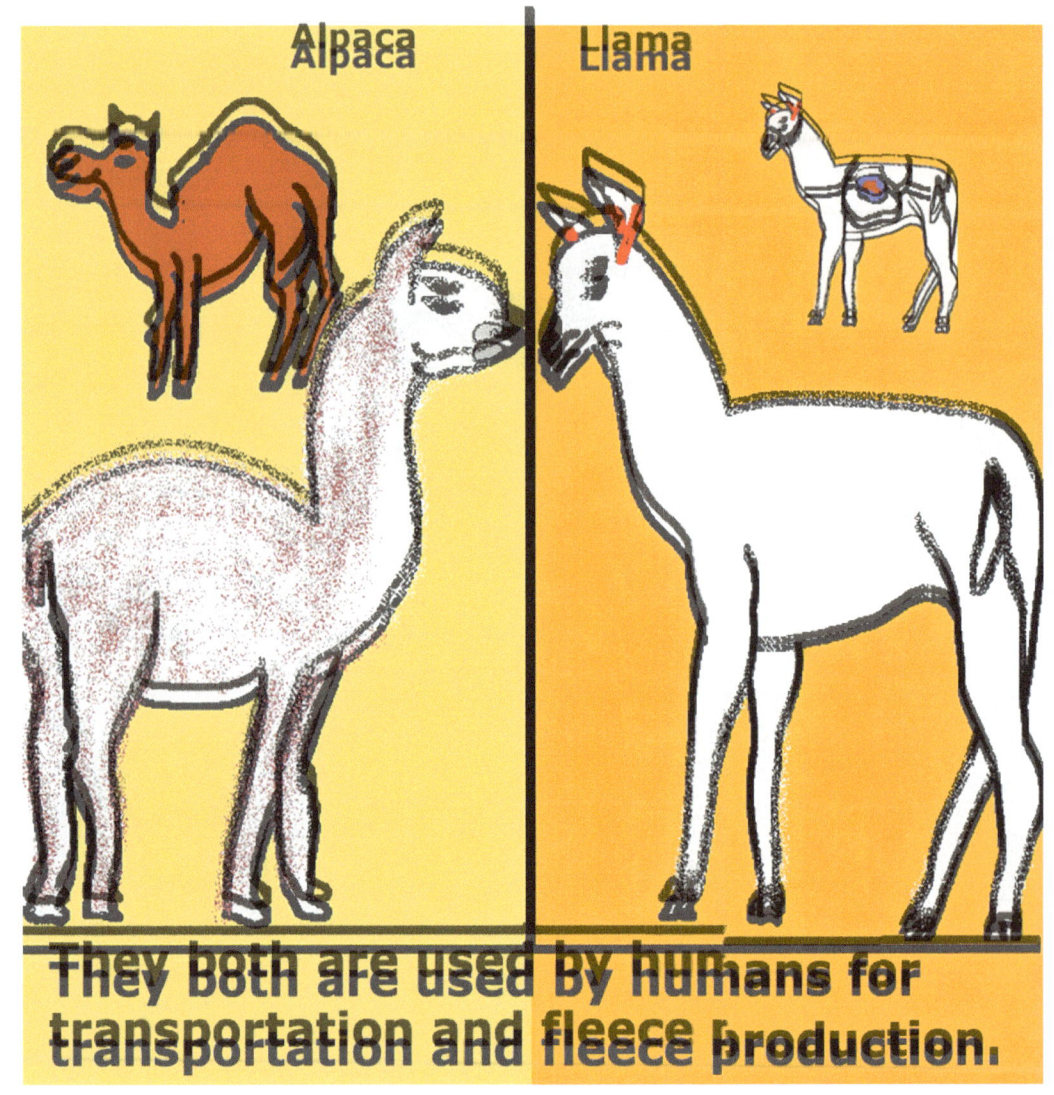

They both are used by humans for transportation and fleece production.

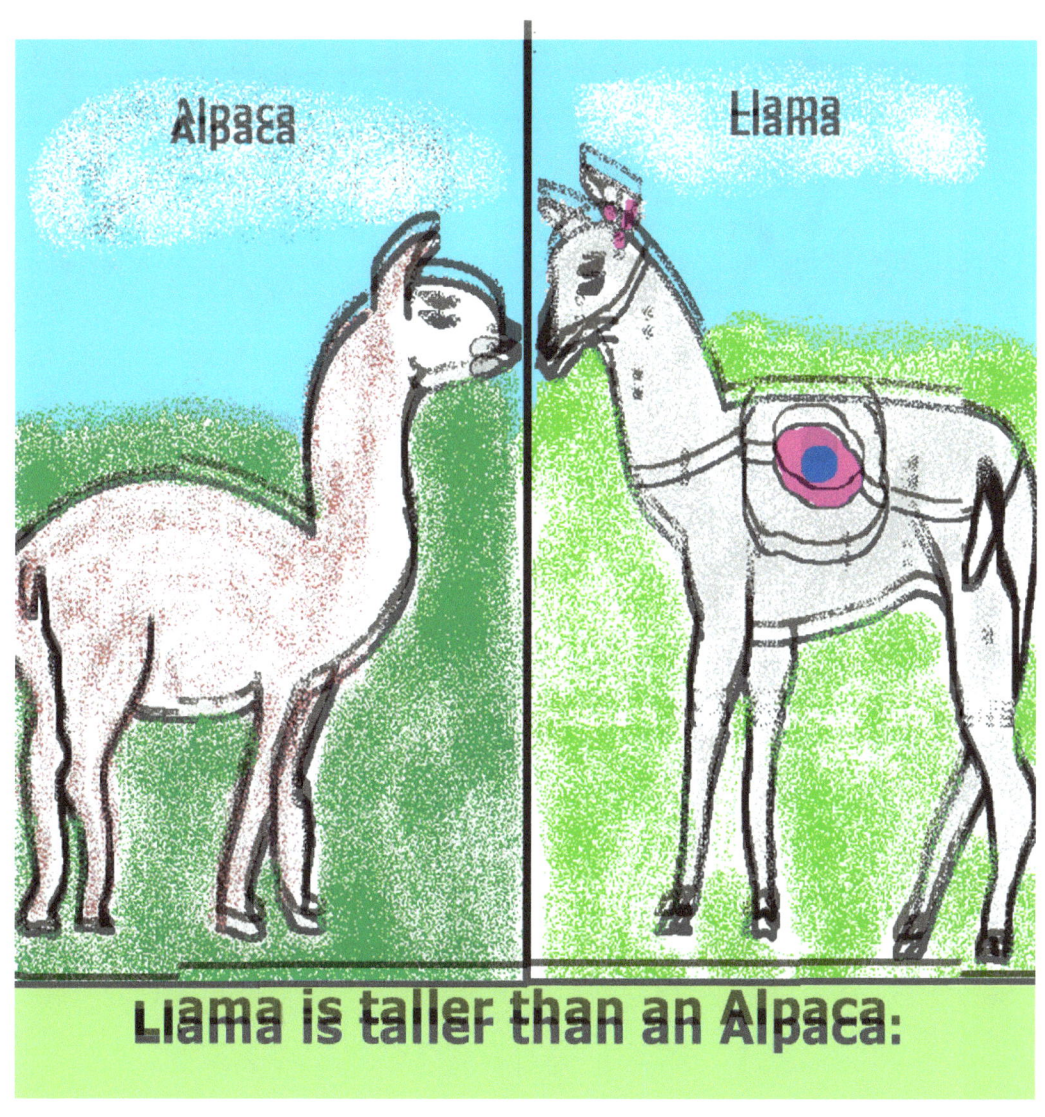

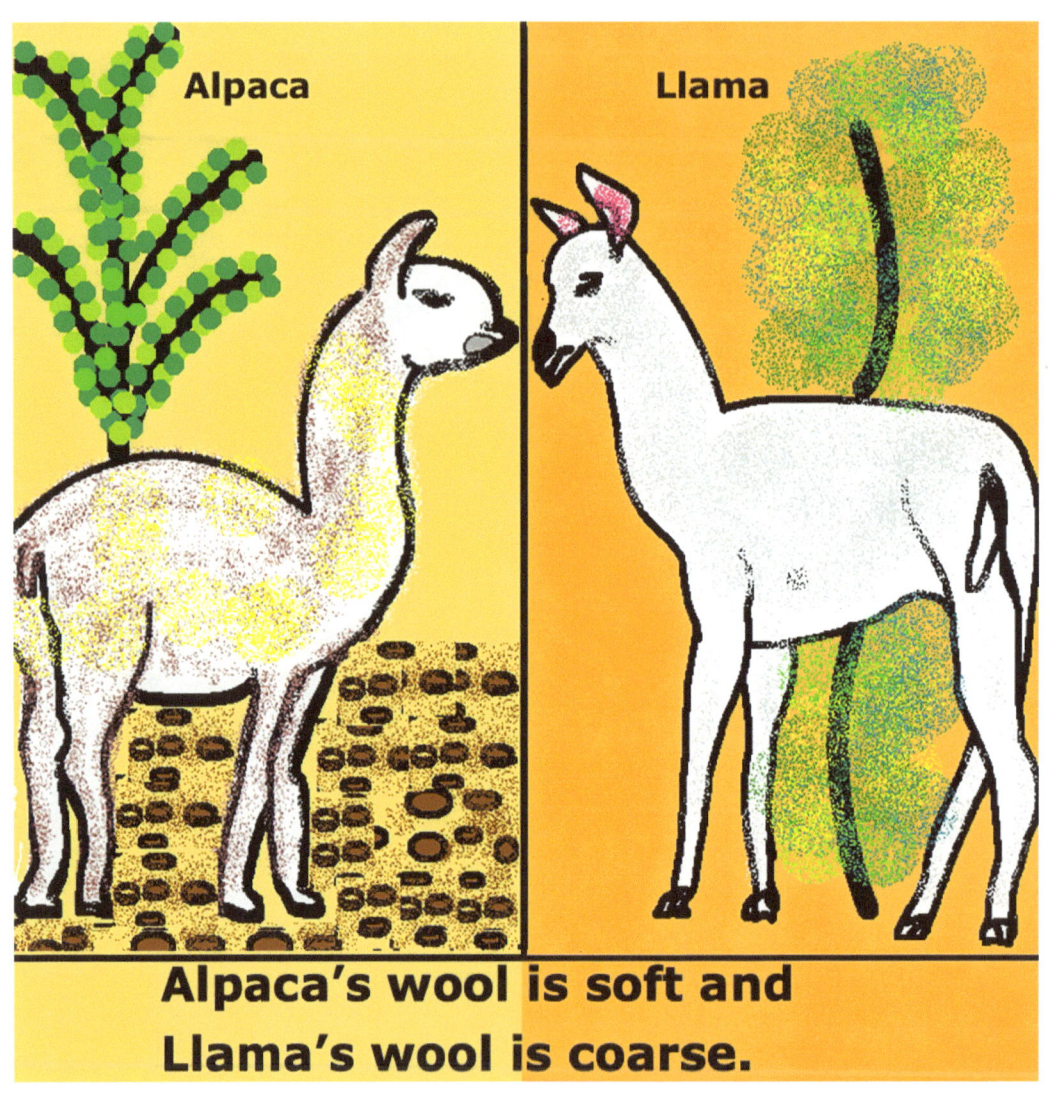

Alpaca's wool is soft and Llama's wool is coarse.

Alpaca

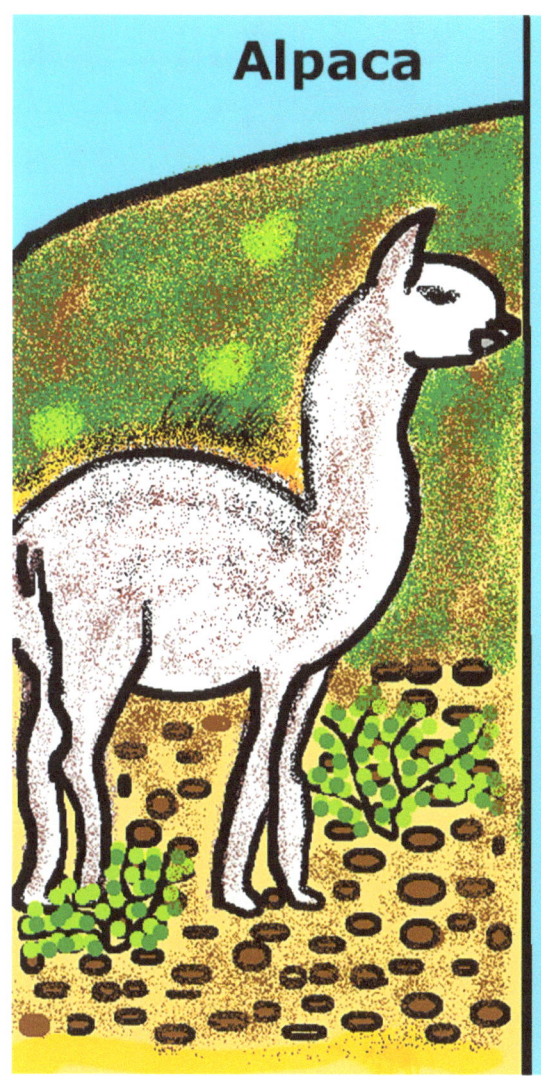

Alpaca is timid.

Llama

Llamas refuse to move if ill treated. They react by spitting and kicking.

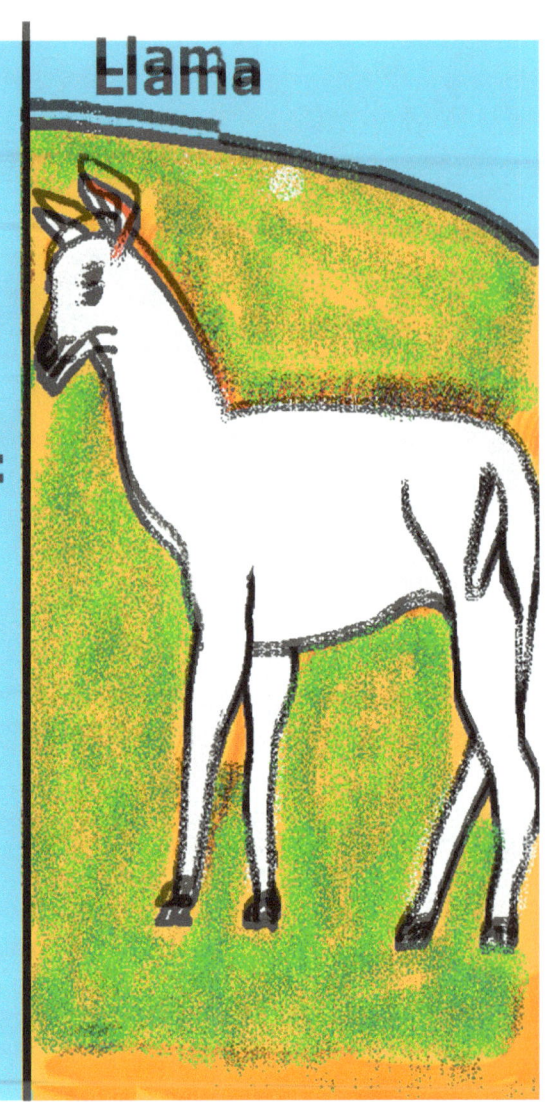

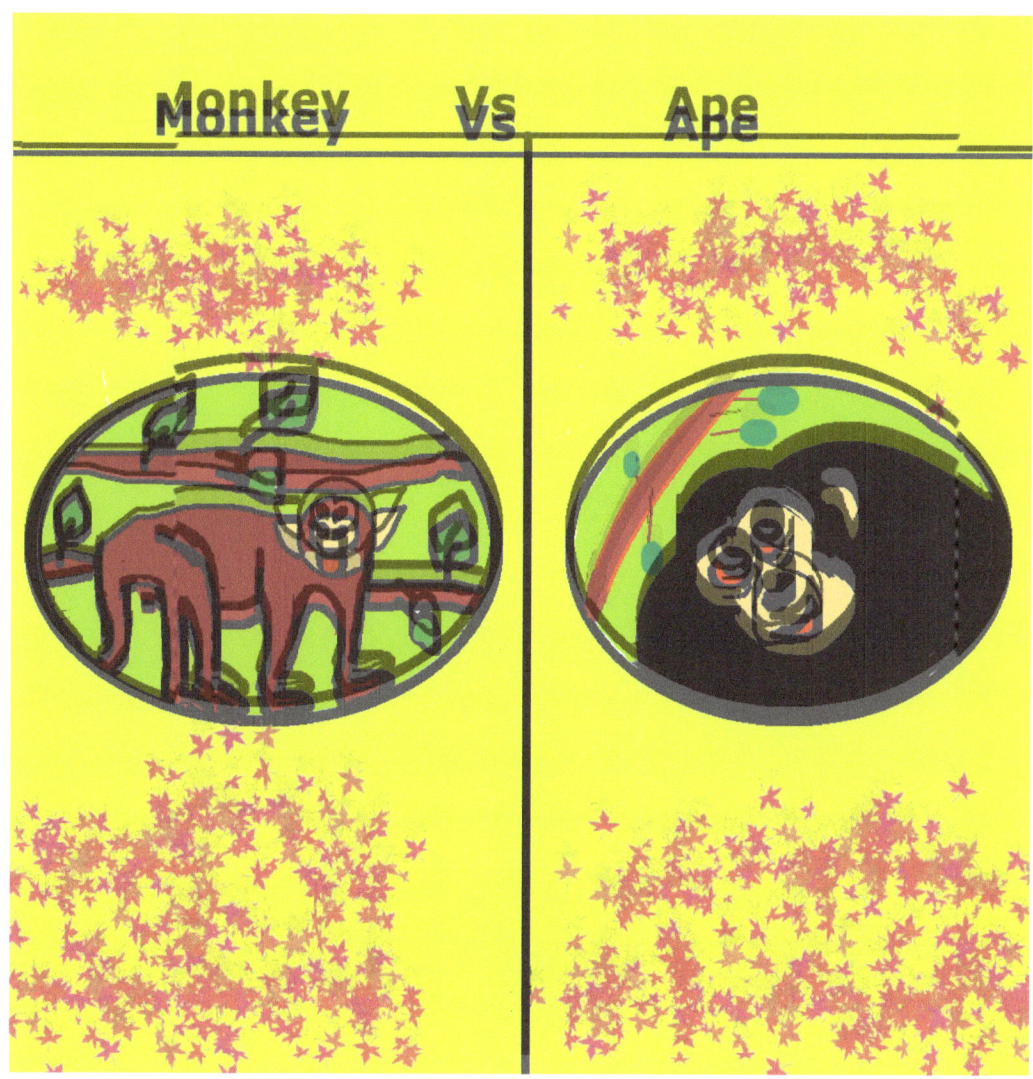

Monkey　　Vs　　Ape

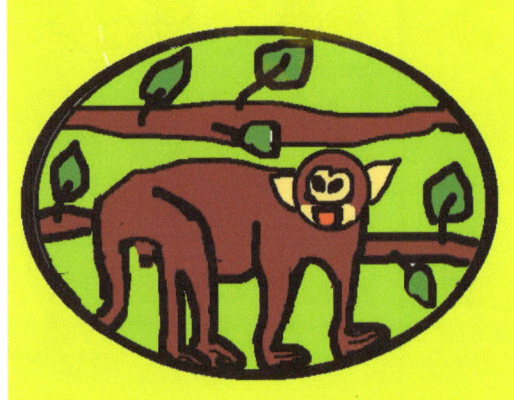 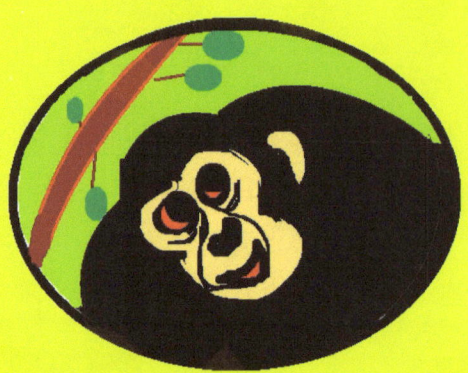

Like humans, monkeys and apes belong to primate family.

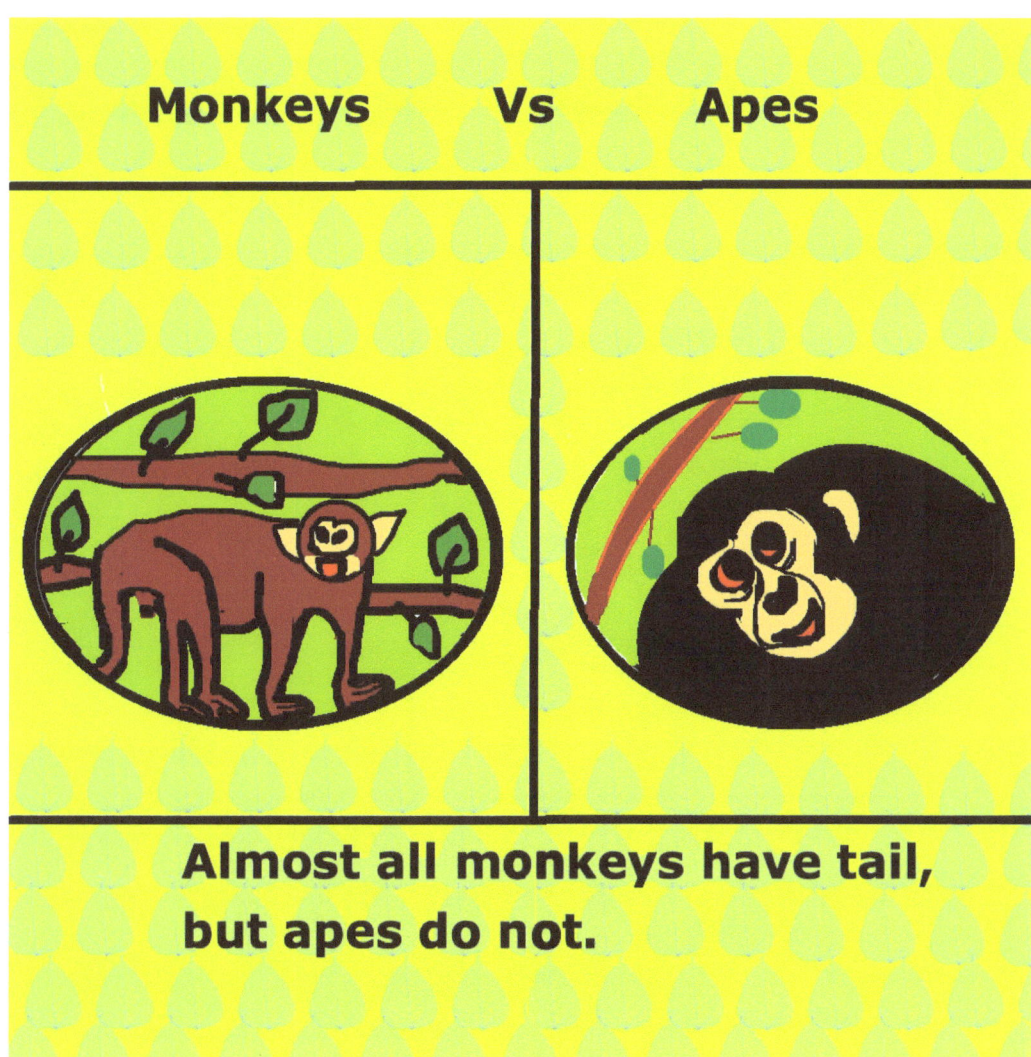

Almost all monkeys have tail, but apes do not.

Monkeys Vs Apes

Monkeys are narrow-chested.
Apes are broad-chested.

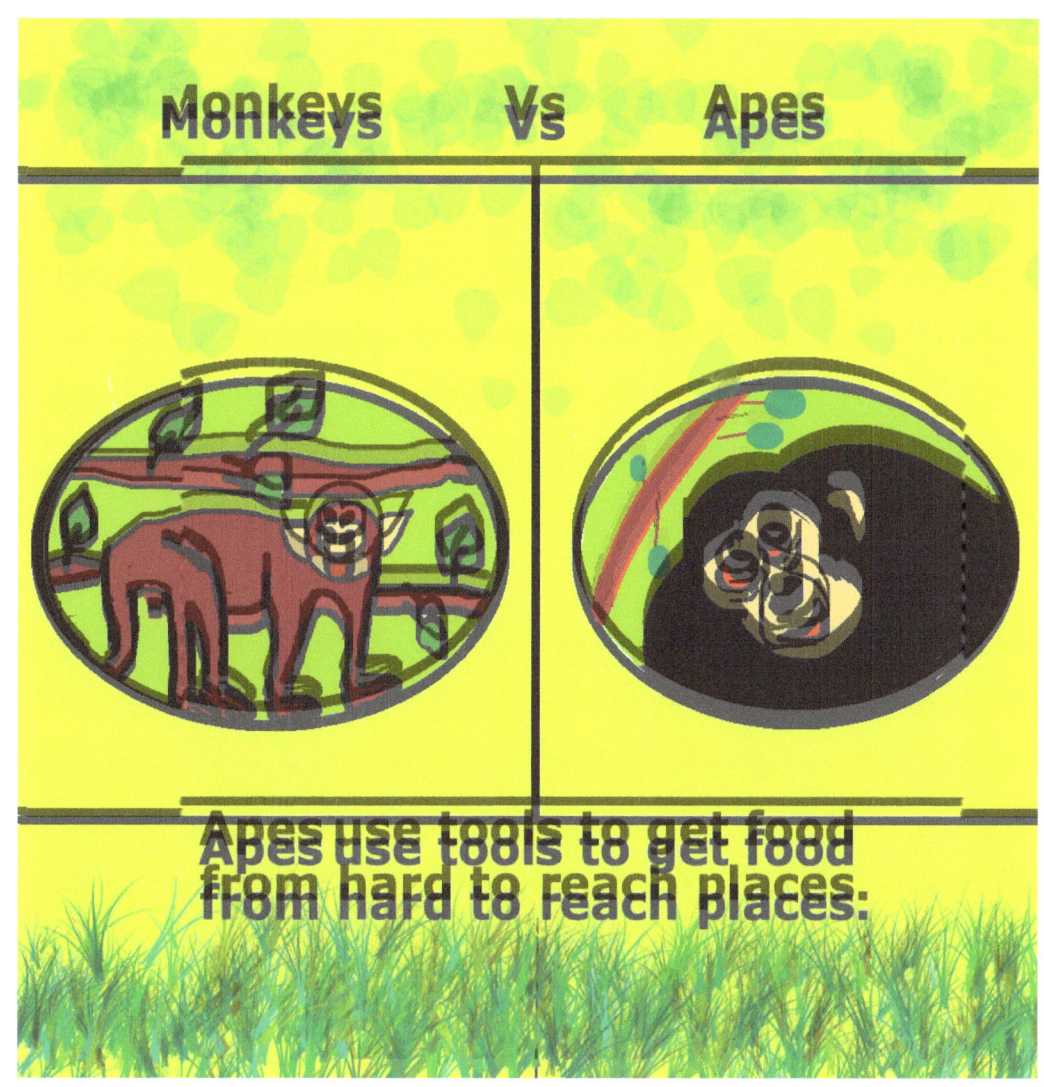

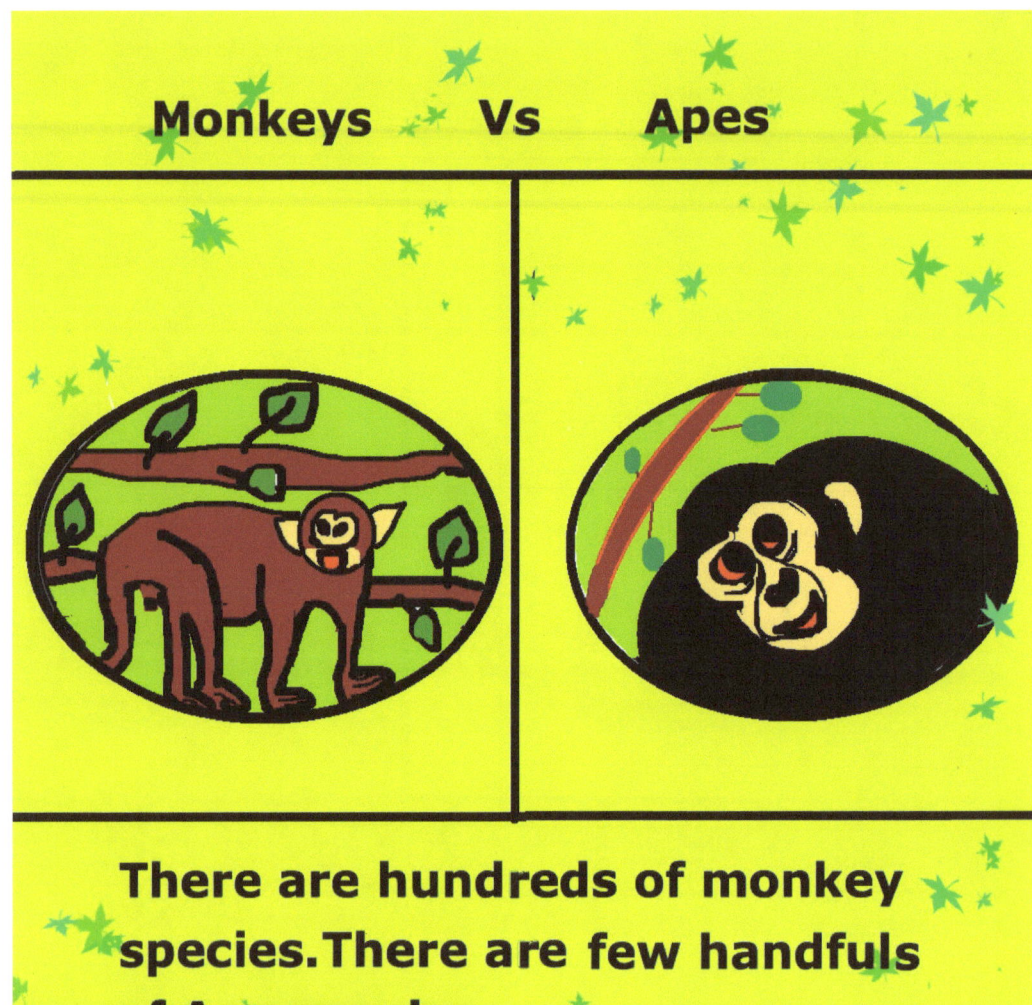

There are hundreds of monkey species. There are few handfuls of Ape species.

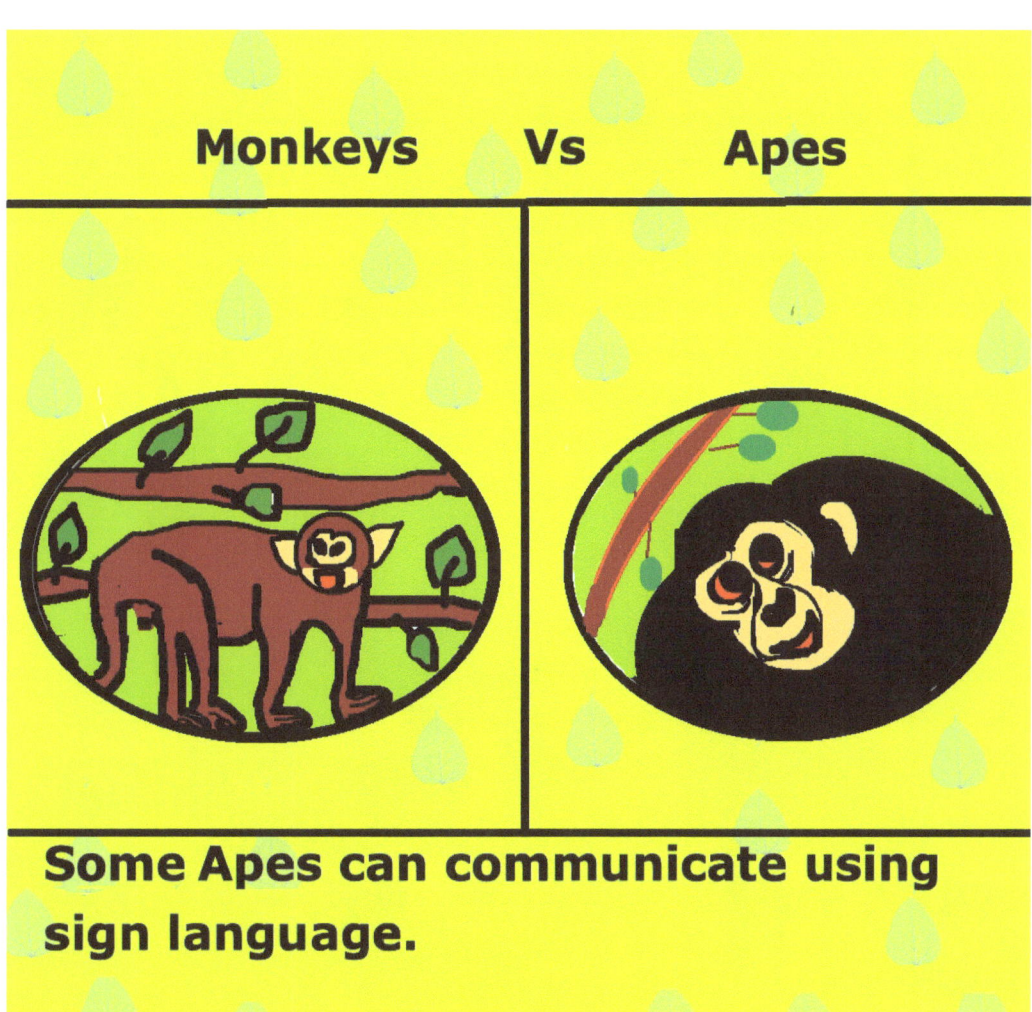

Some Apes can communicate using sign language.

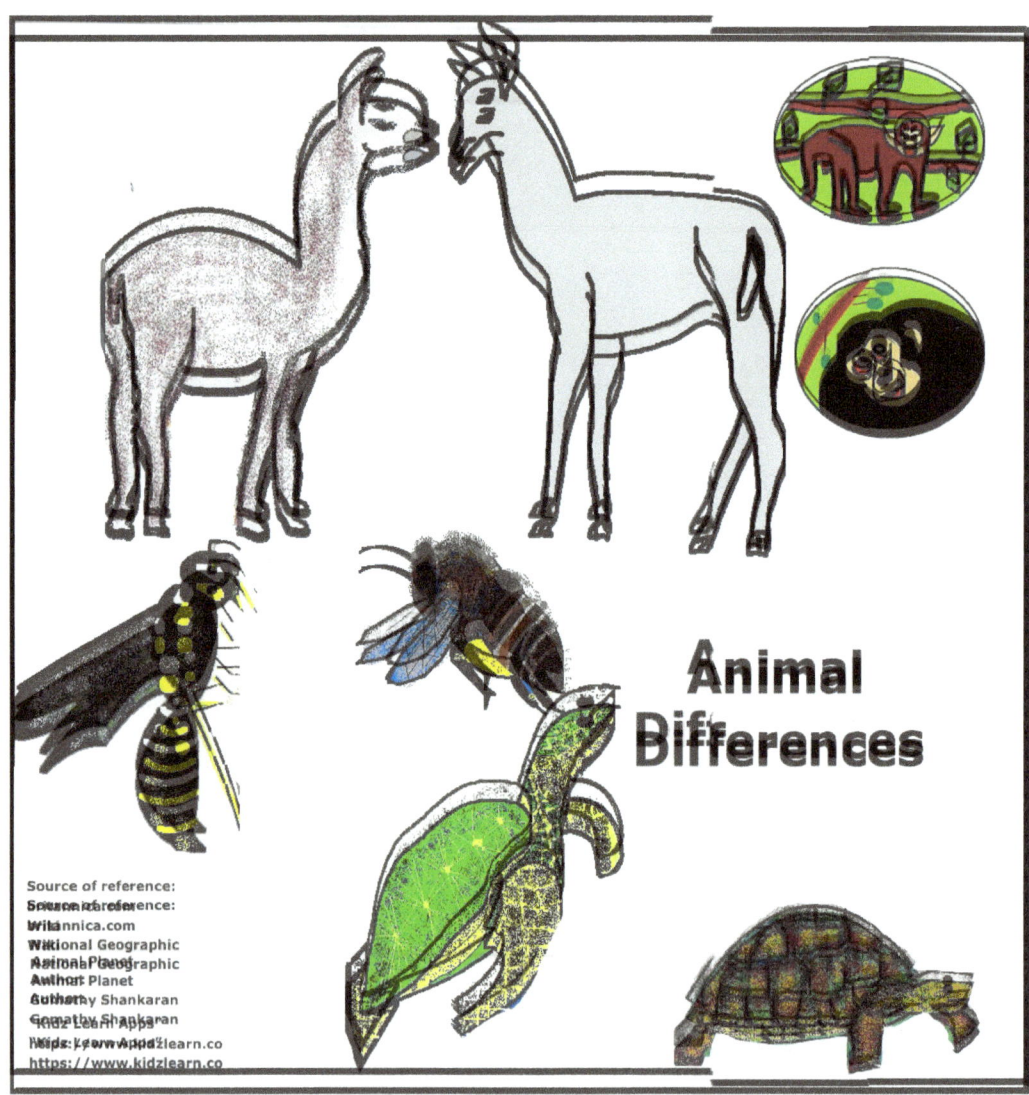

www.ingramcontent.com/pod-product-compliance
Lightning Source LLC
Chambersburg PA
CBHW051939210526
45473CB00006B/2313